GREAT MYSTERIES

Amelia Earhart

OPPOSING VIEWPOINTS®

Look for these and other exciting *Great Mysteries: Opposing Viewpoints* books:

GREAT MYSTERIES

Amelia Earhart

OPPOSING VIEWPOINTS®

by Jane Leder

Greenhaven Press, Inc. P.O. Box 289009, San Diego, California 92128-9009

Library of Congress Cataloging-in-Publication Data

Leder, Jane Mersky.
   Amelia Earhart.

    (Great mysteries : opposing viewpoints)
    Bibliography: p.
    Includes index. *90B4851*
    Summary: Explores the mystery of the disappearance of the famous woman aviator in 1937 while attempting to fly around the world. Was she lost at sea or did she survive?
    1. Earhart, Amelia, 1897-1937—Juvenile literature. 2. Air pilots—United States—Biography—Juvenile literature. [1. Earhart, Amelia, 1897-1937. 2. Air pilots] I. Title. II. Series: Great mysteries (Saint Paul, Minn.)
TL540.E3L43 1989   629.13'092 [B] [92]   89-12028
ISBN 0-89908-070-7

12.95

© Copyright 1989 by Greenhaven Press, Inc.
Produced by Carnival Enterprises

*To all women
who have spread their wings
and flown.*

Contents

Introduction

This book is written for the curious–those who want to explore the mysteries that are everywhere. To be human is to be constantly surrounded by wonderment. How do birds fly? Are ghosts real? Can animals and people communicate? Was King Arthur a real person or a myth? Why did Amelia Earhart disappear? Did history really happen the way we think it did? Where did the world come from? Where is it going?

Great Mysteries: Opposing Viewpoints books are intended to offer the reader an opportunity to explore some of the many mysteries that both trouble and intrigue us. For the span of each book, we want the reader to feel he or she is a scientist investigating the extinction of the dinosaurs, an archaeologist searching for clues to the origin of the great Egyptian pyramids, a psychic detective testing the existence of ESP.

One thing all mysteries have in common is that there is no ready answer. Often there are *many* answers, but none on which even the majority of authorities agrees. *Great Mysteries: Opposing Viewpoints* books introduce intriguing views of the experts, allowing the reader to participate in their explorations, their theories, and their disagreements as they try to explain the mysteries of our world.

But most readers won't want to stop here. These *Great Mysteries: Opposing Viewpoints* aim to stimulate the reader's curiosity. Although truth is often impossible to discover, the search is fascinating. It is up to the reader to examine the evidence, to decide whether the answer is there—or to explore further.

"Penetrating so many secrets, we cease to believe in the unknowable. But there it sits nevertheless, calmly licking its chops."

H.L. Mencken, American essayist

Prologue

Navigation's Greatest Unsolved Mystery?

On July 2, 1937, pilot Amelia Earhart and her navigator Fred Noonan began the longest and most difficult leg of the first around-the-world flight attempted by a woman. The pair took off from Lae, New Guinea, in their twin-engine plane and headed northeast for tiny Howland Island, over 2,500 miles away in the South Pacific.

The Lockheed Electra piloted by Earhart was noisy and shaky. Neither the cockpit where she sat nor the navigator's station in the cabin behind her was very big. After several hours in the plane, Earhart and Noonan probably felt the first muscle cramps. Hours later, they most likely found that nothing they did relieved their sore muscles.

Nineteen or twenty hours into the flight, Earhart and Noonan squirmed for a different reason. They had flown more than 2,500 miles, and they should have been able to see Howland Island.

"We must be on you but cannot see you," Earhart radioed to the Coast Guard cutter *Itasca* anchored off Howland. "Gas is running low. Have been unable to reach you by radio. We are flying at 1,000 feet."

A few minutes later, Earhart radioed that she was

Amelia Earhart, one of the most famous aviators of the twentieth century.

Earhart and her husband, George Putnam, at Newark Airport, New Jersey.

circling but still could not see the island or hear anything from the ship.

Then came Earhart's last known radio message. "We are on the line of position one-five-seven-dash-three-three-seven. Will repeat this message on 6,210 kilocycles. Wait. Listening on 6,210. We are running north and south." Earhart's last message gave a hint of where she might be found, but not a definite position. The crew aboard the *Itasca* waited nervously for more word. There was none. At 8:44 a.m. the outside world heard the last from Amelia Earhart.

Earhart, Noonan, and their plane disappeared without a trace. Their fate remains a puzzle that has never been solved. For over fifty years, people have debated what might have happened. Many Americans have been unwilling to accept the possibility that Earhart ran out of gas and crashed the plane in the Pacific Ocean. Rumors of intrigue surrounding her disappearance have inspired books, television documentaries, and imaginative theories. The fate of Amelia Earhart has become a classic American mystery.

One

Who Was Amelia Earhart?

There are streets and schools named after her throughout the United States. Exhibits of her medals, pictures, and books she wrote appear in a hundred libraries. There is a flower named after her, and a commemorative airmail stamp has been minted in her honor. Millions of people all over the world carry her legend in their hearts. How did Amelia Earhart become so famous? What was she like? What made her look for dangerous challenges that brought her fame and eventually led to her death?

Like most children, the relationship between Amelia's parents helped mold her character. Amelia's parents did not have a happy marriage. Even before Amelia was born, her father felt pressured to make a lot of money. Amelia's mother, Amy Otis Earhart, had been spoiled as she was growing up, and she wanted her husband to take care of her in the same way. Amelia's father was a talented young lawyer who dreamed of reaching the United States Supreme Court. But he went to work for a railroad settling claims because the money was good and the work was steady. Still, money remained a problem. There was not enough to suit the upperclass tastes of

Amelia Earhart's parents, Amy and Edwin.

Amelia's mother. Marriage was difficult for her. Her husband was often away on business, she was unused to housework, and she missed her relatives and friends. Just before Amelia's birth, her mother left Kansas City, Missouri, and returned to her parents' home in Atchison, Kansas, to be more comfortable. Amelia Mary Earhart was born in her grandparents' big white house on a bluff overlooking the Missouri River on July 24, 1898.

When Amelia was born, the money pressures on her father increased. His income depended on settling claims against the railroad for a fee. Money was always in short supply. With the birth of a second daughter, Muriel, two years later, Amelia's father began to feel overwhelmed. He felt cheated because he would never be able to follow his dream of reaching the Supreme Court. He resented that his father-in-law saw him as a failure. He started drinking alcohol to forget his troubles. Amelia's father failed to keep business appointments, neglected his work, and finally suffered a "general nervous breakdown," as his family called it. When Amelia was thirteen, she grabbed a bottle of whiskey and poured it down the sink. Her father saw what she had done and almost hit her. Amelia had little sympathy when her father was fired by the railroad later that year.

The Earhart family moved from one city to the next. Mr. Earhart would find a new job and then lose it because of his drinking. One of his many jobs took the family to Springfield, Missouri. Only after the move did the Earharts find out that the employee Mr. Earhart was to replace had changed his mind about retiring. There was no job. The family was forced to break up temporarily. Mr. Earhart went to Kansas City, Missouri, where he lived with his sister and her family. The railroad refused to hire him again because of his reputation, so he opened his own law office. Amelia, her mother, and sister moved to Chicago, where they lived with old friends from Kansas City. A sensitive young woman, Amelia decided not to make the pressures on her parents worse than they already were. She worked hard and

Amelia, age seven.

Earhart was an excellent student even though she attended six different high schools.

16

"With her stamina, determination and ability to concentrate, who knows what she could have discovered if she had chosen the research laboratory rather than aviation as a career?"

Dr. H.J. Muller, Columbia University

"It took me only a few months to discover that I probably would not make the ideal physician. Though I liked learning all about medicine, particularly the experimental side, visions of its practical application floored me."

Amelia Earhart, *The Fun of It*

After Earhart saw her first airshow, she began to spend all her time at airports, watching pilots and planes.

graduated from high school on time, even though she had attended six different high schools. Amelia had become a very determined young adult.

In 1917 Amelia went to Toronto, Canada, where her sister Muriel was attending college. "There for the first time," Amelia wrote in her book, *The Fun Of It*, "I realized what the World War meant. Instead of new uniforms and brass bands, I saw only the results of a four years' desperate struggle; men without arms and legs, men who were paralyzed, and men who were blind." Amelia decided to stay in Toronto and to become a nurse's aide. She spent months working in a Toronto hospital, doing everything from scrubbing floors to playing tennis with patients.

In 1918 Amelia became interested in airplanes. Some of her patients were pilots, and their stories about aerial dogfights over Europe sparked her curiosity. She began spending her spare time at various airfields around Toronto, watching the planes land and take off. "I absorbed all I could," Amelia wrote. "I remember the sting of the snow on my face as it was blown back from the propellers when the training planes took off on skis." One afternoon, a captain in the Royal Flying Corps stunted for

Amelia and her sister. "At that moment," Amelia wrote in *Last Flight*, "his little red airplane said something to me as it swished by." From then on, most of her free hours were spent at the airfield.

However, it was medicine, not flying, that Amelia decided to pursue. Her experiences as a nurse's aide encouraged her to become a physician. She entered Columbia University in New York City and did very well. But she left Columbia at the end of her first year. "It took me only a few months to discover,"

When Earhart earned her pilot's license in 1922, she became one of a handful of women worldwide who could fly an airplane.

Friendship, the plane in which Earhart first flew across the Atlantic Ocean.

she wrote, "that I probably should not make the ideal physician. Though I liked learning all about medicine, particularly the experimental side, visions of its practical application floored me." Rather than become a doctor, Amelia decided to continue in medical research in California. Her father had stopped drinking and relocated in Los Angeles, where her mother had joined him. Amelia was bent on preventing another parental separation and headed to Los Angeles. She promised herself to return to New York and her own life as she wanted to live it, once she was certain her parents were on steady ground.

Long before the college year began in California, Amelia started to hang around several airfields in the Los Angeles area. At an airshow in Long Beach, Amelia persuaded her father to ask how much it cost to learn to fly. One thousand dollars—too much money. Soon after, Amelia paid a dollar for ten minutes in a plane piloted by Frank Hawks, a pilot who later would break many speed records in the air. The plane lifted over the Hollywood hills, about two or three hundred feet up. Amelia knew at that moment that she had to fly. Flying was daring and adventuresome, especially for a woman. Most women at the time did not even drive automobiles, let alone pilot airplanes.

Now all that stood between Amelia and a pilot's license was a thousand dollars. Amelia went to work at the telephone company in Los Angeles to earn the money and spent her weekends at a small airport. She cut her hair, wore breeches and a leather coat, and blended in with the male pilots and mechanics.

Amelia signed up on credit for flying lessons with Neta Snook, the first woman to graduate from the Curtiss School of Aviation. "Snooky," as Ms. Snook was called, lectured Amelia on the ground, showed her the plane's controls, and named the various parts

Though she was not the pilot, Earhart became the first woman to cross the Atlantic by air in *Friendship*. Afterward, she earned the nickname "Lady Lindy," after Charles Lindbergh.

Earhart's fame created new opportunities. Earhart, shown here with actors Cary Grant and Myrna Loy, consulted on a film they were making about fliers.

Earhart being interviewed upon her arrival at Oakland Airport in California.

of the plane used for training. Finally, seated in the rear cockpit, "Snooky" taught Amelia her basic maneuvers in the air. Amelia got her pilot's license in 1922, making her one of about a dozen licensed women fliers in the world.

A Birthday Gift

For her twenty-fifth birthday later that same year, Amelia's mother and sister helped her buy a sport biplane called a Kinner Canary. Amelia practiced stalls, spins, and forced landings. She wanted to be ready for any emergency. Her practice paid off when, in October 1922, the engine of a borrowed plane failed on takeoff at fifty feet in the air. Amelia turned off the switches and crashed safely into a cabbage patch. She went on to set her first record just a few days later. She set a new altitude mark for women by flying her plane to 14,000 feet, almost three miles.

Amelia's skill as a flier and her confidence as a woman won respect and admiration. Despite her popularity, however, Amelia could not find a paying job in aviation. She worked at several other jobs to help pay the costs of owning an airplane. But in 1924 Amelia was persuaded to sell her Kinner Canary. Her parents had reached the end of their twenty-nine-year marriage, and Mr. Earhart was granted an uncontested divorce. Amelia, her mother, and her sister decided to move back to the East Coast. Amelia bought a Kissel touring car, also yellow like her plane, and drove across the country to Massachusetts. From there, she returned to Columbia University to continue her medical studies but did not finish them. She later told friends that she wanted to be doing something, not preparing for it.

In the next several years, Amelia Earhart taught English and worked as a social worker. Then in 1928, Mrs. Frederick Guest of London, England, decided a woman should cross the Atlantic Ocean by

airplane as Charles Lindbergh had done the year before. Mrs. Guest bought a plane for the flight and named it *Friendship*. However, she was talked out of being a passenger on the flight herself and decided an "American girl with the right image" should be selected.

The reception for Earhart in Culmore, Ireland, in 1932 was for a very special occasion: she had just completed the first solo transatlantic flight by a woman.

Lady Lindy

Amelia Earhart was selected as that American girl. At first, Earhart was disappointed to learn that she would not pilot the plane across the Atlantic. But the promise of the adventure and fame lured her to join the flight. In June 1928 she made headlines and received ticker-tape parades after becoming the first woman to cross the Atlantic in a flight from Newfoundland to Wales. The public considered her a heroine, even though she had only been a passenger on the flight. Earhart got the nickname "Lady Lindy,"

President Herbert Hoover presents a National Geographic Society medal to Earhart for her solo flight across the Atlantic Ocean.

Earhart and her husband, George Putnam.

the female counterpart of Charles Lindbergh.

She lived up to her nickname. Earhart went on to set a long list of flying records. Five years after Lindbergh's historic flight, Earhart was the first woman to make a solo flight across the Atlantic. In 1935 she became the first person to fly solo the 2,400 miles from Hawaii to California and the first to fly alone from Los Angles to Mexico City. From there she set another record by flying nonstop all the way to Newark, New Jersey.

Earhart gained worldwide acclaim. She was in demand as a speaker and endorser of products such as cigarettes (though she did not smoke) and luggage. When she was in Europe, she met kings and princes. Back home in the United States, she dined with President and Mrs. Herbert Hoover at the White House and later with President Franklin D. Roosevelt. Earhart received many commendations, including the Distinguished Flying Cross, before a joint session of Congress in 1932. This award honored outstanding achievement in aviation.

The year before receiving the Distinguished Flying Cross, Earhart married George Putnam. Putnam had proposed five times before Earhart finally accepted. Putnam was twelve years older than Earhart and divorced. Earhart's mother opposed the marriage, but her objections had no influence on Earhart. She and George Putnam were married at his mother's house in Noank, Connecticut, on February 7, 1931. But Earhart herself was still not sold on the idea of marriage. On the morning of the wedding, she handed her fiance a letter, which he called "brutal in its frankness but beautiful in its honesty." "You must know again my reluctance to marry," she wrote. "I feel the move just now as foolish as anything I could do. I know there may be compensations, but have no heart to look ahead..."

One Last Flight

But Earhart had the heart to look ahead to her future. She told a reporter in 1937, "I have a feeling that there is just one more good flight left in my system, and I hope this flight is it." The one more good flight was a flight around the world. A group of male Army pilots had made the first around-the-world flight in 1924. They used three different planes and stayed close to land for safety. Earhart wanted to follow the equator—a more dangerous route over water.

"To me, it was genuinely surprising what a disproportion of attention was given to the woman member of the *Friendship* crew at the expense of the men, who were really responsible for the flight."

Amelia Earhart, *The Fun of It*

"It is great pleasure to come here and share in your honoring of Mrs. Amelia Earhart Putnam. She has shown a splendid courage and skill in flying alone across the Atlantic ocean...She has been modest and good-humored."

President Herbert Hoover

Earhart with General H.C. Pratt and famed aviator Jimmy Doolittle, November 1934.

In 1936, at the Franklin Institute in Philadelphia, Earhart met Orville Wright.
The father of flight was then 65.

Purdue University (where Earhart had been a career counselor for women students) contributed $50,000 toward a plane for Earhart's around-the-world flight. She chose the most advanced non-military plane built in 1936, Lockheed's twin-engined Electra. The plane had a fifty-five-foot wing span and two 500-horsepower engines.

On July 22, 1936, the *Los Angeles Times* published a front-page photograph of Earhart and her new Electra with its official registration mark: NR 16020. The Times priced the plane at $70,000, saying it was "equipped for a possible nonstop flight of 4,500 miles."

The seats in the cabin of the plane had been removed and fuel tanks inserted. The Electra could hold a total of 1,204 gallons of fuel. Its cruising speed was reportedly 180 to 190 MPH, with a top speed of 220 MPH. Cruising altitude was 8,000 feet. In the front of the plane's main cabin a navigation

The new Lockheed Electra, as it was being built, was inspected by Earhart at the factory. This would be the plane for her around-the-world flight.

The team assembled by Earhart for her dramatic flight (from left to right): Paul Mantz, Earhart, Harvey Manning and Fred Noonan.

room was built. When Earhart saw the Electra for the first time, she called it her "flying laboratory."

Paul Mantz, a well-known Hollywood stunt pilot, was the technical director for the project and oversaw the installation of the fuel tanks and other special equipment on board. Even President Roosevelt, a friend of Earhart's, got in on the act by approving government construction of an airstrip on Howland Island, a United States possession. The order by Roosevelt was not just to help Earhart. A runway on Howland Island would aid the United States in keeping an eye on the growing Japanese military power in the Pacific. And Earhart's husband helped raise thousands of dollars to help pay expenses for the 27,000-mile flight.

The around-the-world route was planned from east to west. Two navigators, Fred Noonan and Harvey Manning, would be on board during the more difficult stretches over the Pacific Ocean. On March 17, 1937, Earhart, Mantz (who was going as far as Hawaii), Noonan, and Manning took off from Oakland, California. Only a few hundred people saw the perfect take-off, but a photographer from the San Francisco Chronicle got a picture of the plane passing over the Golden Gate Bridge. The photograph of Earhart's Electra made the front pages of newspapers across the country.

The flight from Oakland to Honolulu went without a hitch. Earhart landed the Electra after fifteen hours and fifty-two minutes flying time. But while taking off from Honolulu on the second leg of the trip, the plane did not gain speed quickly enough. The nose of the plane lurched to the left, then began to swing to the right. Earhart pulled back on the left engine throttle, but her move was too firm. The plane made a sharp, uncontrollable turn while still on the ground, and the landing gear collapsed. None of the three crew members was hurt, but the plane suffered serious damage. The landing gear was smashed, one wing was crippled, and a wing tank was ripped open. Undaunted, Earhart decided to have the damaged Electra fixed and then try again.

The plane was shipped back to the factory in California for repairs that took almost two months. By the time the Electra was ready to be flown again, the weather patterns around the world had changed. A west-to-east route would be better for a late spring departure, so the trip had to be replanned in the opposite direction. The new route was a difficult 29,000 miles, or 2,000 miles longer than the original one. In the meantime, Harry Manning withdrew from the project. Earhart and Noonan would have to face the challenge alone.

Two

How Did Earhart's Last Flight End In Tragedy?

On May 20, 1937, the second flight began as before in Oakland, California. The repaired Electra with Earhart and Fred Noonan aboard headed for Florida. As they landed to refuel at Tucson, Arizona, the left engine burst into flames. Luckily, the damage this time was not serious and was fixed by the next morning. Earhart and Noonan flew to New Orleans the next day; from there, they finished the flight to Miami.

Now began a week of final preparations. The mechanics from Pan American Airlines in Miami did a last tune-up on the plane. Earhart and Noonan waited, trying to stay calm and focused on the flight ahead of them. For Noonan, the around-the-world flight meant a second chance. Though he was an outstanding navigator who had been given many important jobs in his career with Pan American Airlines, he, like Earhart's father, had a drinking problem. He had been fired from the airlines because of his addiction to alcohol.

Earhart had been warned about Noonan. Since he was originally chosen to be the assistant navigator, Earhart did not think there was a great deal to worry

Earhart in her favorite place: the cockpit of an airplane.

The eastward route as flown by Earhart and Noonan on their around-the-world attempt. Neither the plane nor its crew reached Howland Island.

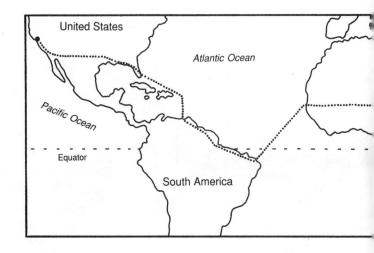

about. When Noonan was sober, he was among the finest airmen in the world. And he promised Earhart that he would not drink during the around-the-world flight. After Harvey Manning left the project, Earhart decided she would not make the flight alone, but with Noonan if he wanted to go along as the solo navigator. When she asked him if he wanted to go, he replied, "I do. I need this flight."

"All the way?" she asked.

"Do you trust me?" he asked.

"I believe in you," she answered.

Earhart herself made the final check of the Electra before the next leg of the flight to Africa. Worried about all the weight the plane had to carry, she decided to remove the 250-foot, trailing-wire antenna from the plane. It was too bulky and too much trouble to reel out and reel in while she was trying to fly the plane. (The antenna was an important part of the plane's emergency radio, and was operated with a telegraph key.) Apparently, neither Earhart nor Noonan was very good with Morse code, and they did not consider that a telegraph key could send out a much clearer signal than the human voice. Besides, they still had a loop antenna

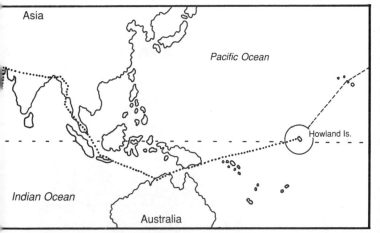

Asia

Pacific Ocean

Indian Ocean

Australia

Howland Is.

"From a navigational aspect, our flights over the desert were more difficult than over water. That was because the maps of the country are very inaccurate and…extremely misleading."

Fred Noonan, after crossing Africa during the around-the-world flight

"I warned AE [Amelia] about the Howland Island leg. With perfect weather conditions, they would have had a good chance to make it. But the weather wasn't perfect; a typhoon had just blown out of the Caroline Islands and they undoubtedly hit plenty of turbulence."

Paul Mantz

on board to be used to contact and to receive voice radio messages from the ground.

Shortly after five o'clock in the morning on June 1, 1937, Earhart and Noonan climbed into the Electra to resume their flight around the world along the equator. Around noon, Noonan alerted Earhart that the plane was too far south of the intended course. Earhart turned the plane back on course and headed for the airport in San Juan, Puerto Rico.

In San Juan the next morning, Earhart learned that the runway was being repaired at their second scheduled stop, Paramaribo, Dutch Guiana, on the northeast coast of South America. She flew instead to Venezuela and waited there until the Paramaribo runway was open again. After flying through heavy rain and strong winds, the fliers arrived in Paramaribo.

The next day came with clear skies, and Earhart and Noonan took off as scheduled for Fortaliza in Brazil, a flight that would cover 960 miles of jungle and 370 miles of ocean. The Electra would cross the equator for the first of four times in the flight.

On June 10 the Electra began a 4,350-mile stretch across Africa. Many of the regions they

In Miami, Noonan and Earhart are greeted by Standard general manager Henry Linam and Pan American Airways manager Harry Drake.

planned to cross had rarely, if ever, been flown over. There were no radio beams to home in on or any lights at the landing fields where they planned to stop for refueling. For Noonan, the task of navigating over Africa was more difficult than navigating over any ocean. The sun and the stars were their only guide.

On to the Pacific

From India, Earhart piloted the Electra south through Indonesia. From Indonesia, the fliers went on to Australia and then to Lae, New Guinea. Only 7,000 miles remained of the 29,000-mile flight. But the next leg was to be the longest and most dangerous of the journey. It would take them 2,556 miles over the Pacific Ocean to tiny Howland Island, located just north of the equator and some 1,900 miles southwest of Hawaii. About half of the flight would be at night, out of sight of land.

Lae was an ideal place to begin. It was the headquarters for the Guinea Airways Company, which flew a Lockheed 10, a plane much like the Electra. Service for Earhart's Electra would be excellent.

Throughout the day after landing in Lae, the mechanics went over the Electra, cleaning the spark plugs and oil filters, changing the engine oil, and running the engines. Earhart was hoping that the mechanics would get everything done so that she and Noonan could leave on July 1. She was feeling pressure from her husband to get to Oakland, California, by July 4 to keep several dates for public appearances that he had made for her.

It became clear, however, that the flight would not get under way on July 1 as Earhart had hoped. The chronometers (or clocks) on the plane could not be set precisely because the exact-time radio signals from the U.S. Navy and the Bureau of Standards had not been picked up. These were

Earhart gained and shared many of her experiences with such aviators as Wiley Post and Roscoe Turner.

Paul Mantz was worried about the longest leg of the flight from Lae, New Guinea, to Howland Island over 4,300 miles of water.

"Her plans all seemed to make reasonable good sense to me except for her plan for navigation between Darwin, Australia, and Howland Island. All of her previous transoceanic flights (and all the earlier legs of this proposed flight) involved flying over or to points where there were operating radio stations on the ground."

Bradford Washburn, explorer/pilot

"Amelia Earhart never intended to land at Howland Island...The field wasn't finished the way it should have been, and no one could have landed with all those birds anyway. There were thousands of them all over that island."

William Galten, a radio operator aboard the *Itasca*

essential for accurate celestial navigation. The weather was also a problem. The direction of the wind, which blew across rather than down the runway, would have forced a dangerous take-off. So the wait continued.

Twenty-five hundred miles away, the U.S. Coast Guard cutter *Itasca* was anchored off Howland Island to help guide Earhart's plan in by radio. The *USS Ontario*, located halfway between Lae and Howland, was to provide weather information.

A Fatal Mistake?

While Earhart and Noonan waited for the plane and conditions to be ready, they discarded nonessential equipment from the Electra to make it as light as possible. They kept only emergency rations, fresh water, a two-person rubber raft, life belts, flares, a pistol, and a signal kit. "We have even discarded as much personal property as we can decently get along without and henceforth propose to travel lighter than ever before," wrote Earhart. "All Fred has is a small tin case which he picked up in Africa. I notice it still rattles, so it cannot be packed very full."

Earhart and Noonan took off for Howland Island at mid-morning on July 2 and presumably headed northeast toward Howland. A direct route would have taken them by the New Britain, Solomon, Nukumanu, and Gilbert Island groups as well as by the *USS Ontario*. They would make an early-morning arrival at Howland after almost a day in the air. For Earhart to be able to hit her target the weather would have to be clear enough for Noonan to take his fixes from the stars at night, and from the sun

Earhart as she appeared in front of her Lockheed Electra before her disappearance in July 1937.

Whenever Earhart set a new flying record, she was always met with enthusiastic crowds.

during the day. Once over the ocean and more than 500 miles out, Earhart would no longer be able to contact Lae by radio. To get a radio bearing from Howland, she would have to fly all night and never go off course. Then she could home in on signals from the *Itasca*. If she had not removed the trailing-wire antenna from the plane before she left Miami, she would have been able to contact the *Itasca* much farther away than with just the loop antenna left on board.

To make matters worse, there was much confusion over the direction finder (DF) that had been installed on Howland Island. The direction finder was a major breakthrough in aviation. Air crews could be pointed to their destination by tuning their DF radio to a certain frequency and lining up their loop antenna, a type of direction finder. With a DF on the ground an operator could tune in to an aircraft's radio transmissions, get a bearing, and relay that information to the crew by voice. To use a DF correctly, Earhart would have to transmit at a certain frequency, and the operator on the ground would have to transmit for about two minutes. But either Earhart did not know that a DF had been installed on Howland Island or she didn't know how to use hers properly.

Radio Problems

One hour after takeoff, Earhart radioed the Lae radio operator, Harry Balfour. Four hours later, she reported to Balfour again. She was cruising at 10,000 feet but had run into thick banks of clouds and was reducing her altitude. Shortly after sunset, Earhart called in again to tell Balfour that she was flying at 7,000 feet and making 150 knots. She also said that she was going to change to another frequency on the radio, the frequency best received during the evening hours (3,105 kilocycles). Balfour immediately urged Earhart not to switch because her signal was still very strong. Either she did not hear him or she ignored his advice, and Balfour never heard from Earhart again. In fact, Earhart never had two-way radio communication with anyone again.

The *Ontario*, anchored between Lae and Howland, had not heard from Earhart at all. The crew was worried. Either she was far off course and could not be heard, or she was lost. Aboard the *Itasca*, the radio room chief looked at the clock. It was 1:48 in the morning at Howland; Earhart had been airborne for more than 14 hours. Chief Radioman Leo Bellarts pressed his earphones closer as Earhart's voice drifted in, then faded out. All he heard was, "Cloudy weather, cloudy." But at least it was Earhart. An hour later, Earhart was back. "*Itasca* from Earhart. *Itasca* broadcast on 3,105 kilocycles on hour and half hour—repeat—broadcast on 3,105 kilocycles on hour and half hour. Overcast."

"With the extra gas tanks I put aboard her plane, she had a range of well over 4,000 miles. She could have flown a good part of the way toward Howland and still would have had enough fuel to make Saipan."

Paul Mantz

"The Electra would have run out of fuel far short [of Saipan]."

Vincent Loomis, *Amelia Earhart: The Final Story*

Bellarts transmitted by Morse code, "What is your position? When do you expect to arrive at Howland?"

Then he spoke into the microphone. "What is your position? When do you expect to arrive at Howland?"

There was only silence. If Earhart was more than 200 miles away, voice signals on 3,105 kilocycles would have been weak at best. The only thing to do was to wait.

A little more than an hour later, Bellarts received more voice signals. But they were garbled. He could barely hear Earhart, and she didn't respond to his transmissions.

Frank Ciprianti was handling the DF antenna on Howland. He heard Earhart and tried to get her to stay on long enough to get a bearing. She didn't cooperate.

"Give me the weather! I've got to have the weather!" Earhart's voice came through the radio

One of the last photos taken of Earhart and Noonan (far right) on New Guinea before the fateful Pacific flight.

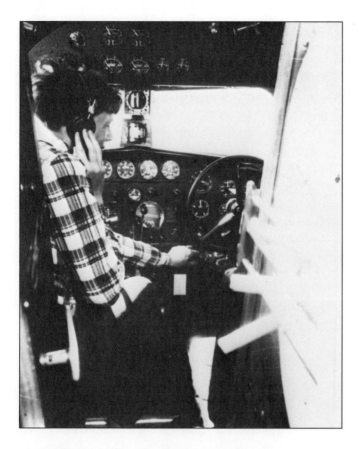

Neither Earhart nor Noonan were very experienced at using the radio equipment aboard the Electra, and they had difficulty using their direction finder.

on the *Itasca*. She sounded very tense.

A radioman tried to reply. He sent the weather on every telegraph channel he had and then repeated it on all voice channels. There was no response from Earhart.

Where Was She?

Over eighteen hours into the flight, Earhart was back on the *Itasca's* radio, this time a little clearer. "Please take bearing on us and report in half hour. I will make noise in microphone. About one hundred miles out. Position doubtful."

The radiomen aboard the *Itasca* were extremely worried and frustrated. They had no idea what Earhart was doing. The radio frequency she was

The Coast Guard cutter *Itasca* was sent to Howland to help guide Earhart's plane to the tiny island.

using was almost impossible for getting a bearing. And she wouldn't stay on the radio for the two minutes needed for the radiomen to relay their location to Earhart. It was as if Earhart had no idea what she was doing or that she was becoming confused.

The radiomen decided to try to get Earhart to change radio frequencies. At 6:18 a.m. Bellarts radioed, "Earhart from *Itasca*. Cannot take bearing on 3,105 very good. Please send on 500 or do you wish to take bearing on us? Go ahead, please."

Earhart did not respond. The radiomen did not know that the antenna she needed to transmit on 500 kilocycles had been left behind in Miami.

Two hours had passed since Earhart's last message. She was long overdue. Suddenly her voice came over loud and clear on the speakers. "We must be on you but cannot see you but gas is running low. Have been unable to reach you by radio. We are flying at 1,000 feet."

Sixteen minutes later she was back. "We are circling but cannot see the island. Cannot hear you. Go ahead on 7,500 kilocycles with long count either now or on scheduled time on half hour."

The crew was frantic. There was not a ship or a DF antenna able to take a bearing on 7,500 kilocycles. Bellarts tapped out a series of Morse code homing signals.

"We received your signals but unable to get minimum," Earhart radioed. "Please take bearings on us and answer on 3,105 kilocycles with voice."

Earhart's transmission didn't last long enough for either Bellarts or Ciprianti on Howland to get a bearing on her. She seemed completely confused and unable to use her radios properly.

At 8:44 a.m. Earhart radioed her final message. "We are on the line of position one-five-seven dash three-three-seven. Will repeat this message on 6,210 kilocycles. Wait. Listening on 6,210. We are running north and south."

The one-five-seven dash three-three-seven apparently represented a sun line (a navigational direction) that Noonan had made. But he could not determine where they were along that line. They were running "north and south" to try to find out. It was like hiking on the right trail but not knowing whether the campsite is behind or ahead, or how far.

The radiomen aboard the *Itasca* waited for more word from Earhart. Nothing. Crewmen on the ship and on Howland scanned the horizon for the plane. Nothing.

At 10:00 a.m. the commander of the *Itasca* ordered the ship to begin a search northwest of Howland.

Three

How Did the U.S. Government React?

"Lady Lindy Lost!" "Earhart Disappears." "Earhart Lost in Pacific."

Amelia Earhart, Fred Noonan, and their plane were lost somewhere in the midst of 450,000 square miles in the South Pacific. The United States Navy, under orders from President Roosevelt, was determined to find them. In addition to the *Itasca*, the navy sent the aircraft carrier *Lexington* and half a dozen other ships to the Howland area. The ships and planes would search for sixteen days and would cover an area of more than 250,000 square miles.

The Japanese controlled many of the islands in the South Pacific, including the Marshalls. In 1920 the League of Nations awarded Japan a limited mandate to rule over the Marshalls and other islands. The Mandated Islands, as they were called, were not to be used for any kind of military activity and construction. However, the Japanese had ignored the League of Nations' mandate and begun to use many of the islands for military purposes. When the United States government asked the Japanese to allow American ships and planes to enter the Marshall Islands, Japan refused, saying they would conduct their own search

The disappearance of Amelia Earhart, one of America's most popular heroes,
sent shockwaves around the nation.

"In regard to the search for the remains of the Earhart plane in our mandate territory, our Imperial national will have all the vessels and fishing boats in the area make every possible effort to search for the remains."

Isoroku Yamamoto, Vice Minister, Ministry of the Navy, Japan

"If Amelia and Fred were taken prisoners, the Japanese could never let them go."

Fred Goerner, *The Search for Amelia Earhart*

for Earhart and Noonan. The United States trusted the Japanese and agreed not to search near Japanese-mandated territory.

Commander Warner Keith Thompson of the *Itasca* was confident that he would find the fliers. Even though Earhart was having radio trouble, he believed that Noonan could still find Howland Island. Thompson ordered that radio transmissions be continued around the clock. If Earhart was using fuel at the rate of fifty gallons per hour, she would have enough fuel left for two hours of flying time. If she was using fuel at just under forty-five gallons per hour, Earhart could stay in the air trying to find some island until about noon. The Gilbert, Marshall, Caroline and Mariana Islands were all possible landing spots. According to Earhart's husband, who was very familiar with emergency plans, the Electra could stay afloat indefinitely. The plane's empty fuel tanks, Putnam said, would give them buoyancy. "Besides," he wired in a telegram from San Francisco, "they have all the emergency equipment they'll need—everything."

The Search Begins

By noon Earhart had not reached Howland. The *Itasca* listened for her radio signals on 3,105 and 500 kilocycles, because everyone aboard the ship believed the plane's radio was powered by battery and that the antenna could be used from on top of the wing of the plane in the water.

The engineers who built the Electra were contacted to find out whether the Electra's radio could operate if the plane were floating. Their answer was discouraging. The Electra's radio needed the right engine for power and could not operate if it were on the water. Now everyone hoped that the plane had landed on land.

The *Itasca* searched an area of 9,500 square miles and found no sign of the plane or the fliers. None of

The last time George Putnam saw his wife alive was in Miami on June 1.

A rare photograph of
Earhart's Lockheed Electra
in flight, 1937.

the other ships or planes turned up a trace, either. The search cost $4 million and was perhaps the most intensive air and sea search in United States history. On July 19, 1937, the navy released the *Itasca* from any further search.

Navy officials concluded that Earhart and Noonan had been forced to ditch the Electra in the ocean and that they had probably gone down with the plane. Many others agreed. Finding tiny Howland Island would have required a perfect route and the best of communication. There were obviously many things that went wrong during this most difficult leg of Earhart's attempt at an around-the-world flight.

However, the American public refused to believe that Earhart and Noonan were dead. Newspapers and radio stations across the country began to relay strange details of the search, convincing Americans that drowning was not the only possibility.

Crewmen on one of the search ships had sighted what they thought might be green flares. Earhart's rubber raft did have emergency flares, and twenty-five witnesses said they saw flares on the northern horizon. The *Itasca*, before being called off the search, went to investigate in the direction where the flares had been sighted. The commander also asked the other ships in the area if they had seen the flares. The answers were all negative. The navy concluded that the lights were just a meteor shower.

Phantom Signals

For several days after Earhart's disappearance, amateur and professional radio operators from Honolulu to Cincinnati reported hearing SOS signals from Earhart. If she had landed on land and were using her radio, it was possible that her signals had bounced back and forth across thousands of miles.

Earhart dining in a hangar with well-wishers during her around-the-world flight.

Earhart and Noonan were lost in thousands of square miles of the South Pacific.
This satellite photograph of the Marshall Islands reveals just how vast
the search area was where the tiny plane went down.

Yet none of the official radio operators in the Pacific picked up any SOS signals. And officials found that one civilian who said that he had picked up signals from Earhart had actually been listening to a radio dramatization of the last flight on commercial radio.

Desperate to find his wife, George Putnam turned to a friend of the missing pilot, Jacqueline Cochran, who was said to have powers of extrasensory perception (ESP). Cochran lived in Los Angeles, and Putnam went to her apartment and begged her to help him find Earhart. Cochran agreed and said she "saw" the Electra on the water in the search area. She told Putnam that Earhart was unhurt but that Noonan had fractured his forehead. Cochran named the *Itasca* as one of the ships involved in the search, claiming never to have heard the name before.

Jacqueline Cochran "followed" the course of the Electra for two days. U.S. Navy ships and planes searched the area where she "saw" the plane drifting. They found nothing. On the third day, according to Cochran, the plane sank.

Hoaxes and Sensationalism

Notes in bottles and messages carved on driftwood were also found after Earhart's disappearance. All of them proved to be hoaxes. Over the years, people's imaginations worked in other ways. Some said that Earhart had been on a spying mission for President Roosevelt and was captured by the Japanese military. Others speculated that Earhart and Noonan were secret lovers who escaped to a desert island. Still others concluded that after the crash Earhart had lost her memory and gone to Japan, where she became a prostitute.

In 1943 RKO Studios encouraged those who said that Earhart had been on a spying mission by making a movie called *Flight for Freedom*. Rosalind Russell played the role of a famous pilot named Tonie Carter. In the movie, Carter plans a flight around the world

Fleet Admiral Chester W. Nimitz (left) and Rear Admiral Forrest P. Sherman (right) chatting with Secretary of the Navy James V. Forrestal during an inspection of the Pacific Fleet. The build-up of the Japanese Imperial Navy in the South Pacific was of great interest to the United States government before World War II.

and agrees to help the United States by making a secret landing at a Pacific island to give search planes a chance to look at Japan's military bases. Just before taking off, however, Carter discovers that the Japanese have learned of her plan and intend to intercept her themselves. At the last minute, Carter ditches the plane into the ocean, allowing the search to continue. The film ends with Tonie Carter and her navigator/fiance living happily ever after. George Putnam sued RKO Films over the movie and settled out of court.

Amy Otis Earhart, Earhart's mother, fueled the spy theory. In 1954 she reported that she believed Earhart had been on a secret spy mission for the United States government. She also told the press that Earhart had been captured by the Japanese and was taken to Tokyo where she was killed, although Mrs. Earhart had no proof for her theory.

At the end of World War II, the Navy Department made a final announcement about Earhart's disappearance. She had not been sent on a spy mission. Her plane had not been shot down by the Japanese. She had not been captured, held as a prisoner, or shot as a spy.

Despite this official announcement, rumors about the disappearance of Amelia Earhart have continued to this day.

"A police inspector at Saipan when Amelia Earhart disappeared on a Pacific flight in 1937 rejected today assertions that the American aviatrix and her navigator were executed by the Japanese."

Associated Press, November 14, 1960

"Amelia Earhart and Fred Noonan were the first prisoners of war and casualties in a conflict yet to come."

Vincent Loomis, *Amelia Earhart: The Final Story*

Four

Was Earhart a Spy?

On May 27, 1960, the *San Mateo Times* in California printed an article about a woman who had seen two American fliers, a man and a woman, on Saipan Island in the Pacific in 1937. The description given by the woman, Josephine Blanco Akiyama, fit Amelia Earhart and Fred Noonan. Akiyama said she was riding her bicycle down the beach road on the island of Saipan, located 1,500 miles north of Lae, New Guinea. As she neared the gate of the secret Japanese seaplane base at Tanapag Harbor, Akiyama saw a large, two-motored plane fly overhead and then disappear near the harbor. When she reached the beach area, she found a large group of people gathered around two white people. They both looked like men, but someone told her that one of them was a woman. Before Japanese guards took the pair away, Akiyama noticed that the man had hurt his head.

Akiyama's story caused quite a sensation. There were those who were certain that the people she had seen could not have been Earhart and Noonan. How could they have flown so far off course and landed in the harbor of Saipan? Others were curious enough to start an investigation. One of these investigations

Earhart and Noonan were photographed everywhere they landed on their global attempt. This was taken in Brazil.

The investigation led by CBS newsman Fred Goerner concluded that Earhart and Noonan had been captured by the Japanese Navy and taken to the island of Saipan.

lasted six years and included four trips to Saipan. These trips were led by Columbia Broadcasting System (CBS) radio broadcaster Fred Goerner, and backed first by CBS and later by the Scripps League of Newspapers, the *San Mateo Times*, and the Associated Press. The conclusion reached by the investigation and detailed in Goerner's 1966 book, *The Search for Amelia Earhart*, shocked the American public: Earhart had been on a spy mission for the United States to see if the Japanese were preparing to take military control of the Pacific.

The Japanese Theory

In 1937 Japan controlled all but three of the Pacific islands north of the equator. The Japanese landing fields and seaplane bases on those islands could be used for military aircraft, posing a threat to the United States. The United States needed bases of its own, but the only islands close enough to the ones controlled by the Japanese were Howland, Baker, and Jarvis. The United States government sought to disguise the building of military landing fields on these islands.

According to Goerner's theory, that is where Earhart came in. She was convinced to change her flight plans and refuel on Howland Island. That gave the United States an excuse to build landing fields there that could be used first for Earhart's flight and later as a military base in defense against the Japanese. And if Earhart's flight succeeded, the American public most likely would have supported

A detail of the South Pacific where Earhart and Noonan were lost. The cross shows where Goerner believes they ended up—Saipan.

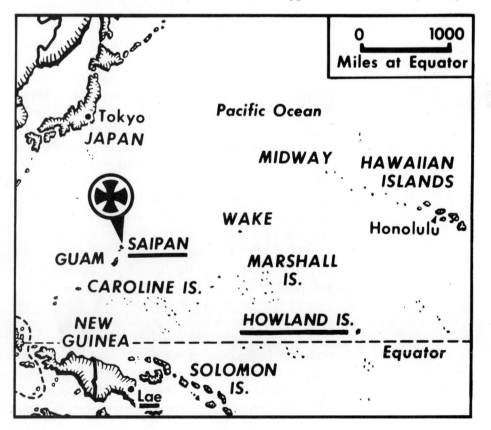

the building of other island landing fields on Jarvis and Baker Islands. Since Earhart disappeared, the United States never constructed those military bases.

During the Goerner team's first visit to Saipan in 1960, they decided to search the bottom of Tanapag Harbor for the missing Earhart plane. Divers returned with a hundred pounds or more of wreckage. The wreckage was covered with algae and coral and was completely unrecognizable. After pounding some of the wreckage with a hammer, a big piece of coral broke loose. What remained looked like a starter mechanism from an airplane. A second dive produced what appeared to be a generator with the serial numbers NK 17999. Goerner sent a telegram that night to Paul Mantz, the technical director for Earhart's around-the-world flight, asking whether the serial numbers had any connection with Earhart's plane. Taking the evidence with them, Goerner and his team returned to the United States.

The initial reports about the generator were promising. At a news conference on July 1, 1960, Paul Mantz announced that the generator "looks exactly like the generator I put aboard Earhart's plane." Reporters ran to telephones, and photographers took photographs of Mantz holding the now-famous generator. Hundreds of newspapers carried the story: "Saipan Generator Believed Earhart's." "Generator Clue to Missing Aviatrix." "Earhart's Generator Believed Found." The next day, mechanics who worked for Mantz broke the generator down piece by piece. They finally got the bearings free and found more number and letter combinations. The combinations were immediately sent to the manufacturer for identification.

The excitement mounted. Mantz and Goerner prepared for another news conference. Mantz had decided that he could be even more definite about the generator. "I'll give a thousand dollars to anyone who can prove the generator found at Saipan is not identical to the one I installed aboard Amelia Earhart's plane," he announced. "It matches perfectly in every respect." As Mantz and Goerner headed out of the news conference, they were handed a news bulletin. It was a serious setback. The Bendix Aviation Corporation had traced the bearings from the generator to a firm in Japan!

Piecing together other information, the Goerner team considered the possibility that Earhart did not land in Saipan, even if she and her plane eventually ended up there. Then Goerner came across an article about Earhart that encouraged this new line of thought.

The article, "Amelia Earhart—College Head Thinks Flier is Jap Captive," was written by Dr. M.L. Brittain, a civilian guest aboard the battleship *Colorado* in June and July of 1937. He described a radiogram he had seen from President Roosevelt to the *Colorado*, received after Earhart's disappearance. The president requested that the ship proceed toward Howland Island. Brittain and members of the crew discussed the rumors that the U.S. government had sent spies to see whether the Japanese were building up their military strength in the Marshall Islands. Brittain "got a very definite feeling that Amelia Earhart had some sort of understanding with officials of the government that the last part of her flight around-the-world would be over those Japanese islands."

Eyewitness Accounts

On his second trip to Saipan, Goerner interviewed a woman who, as a young girl, had lived with her father and mother next to the facility where the Japanese secret police housed political prisoners. Matilde Nicholas claimed that she had seen the white woman whom the Japanese called the "flier and spy." Each day, Nicholas said, the white woman would come out into the yard and walk around.

Earhart's mother Amy did not believe her daughter was lost at sea.

Garapan City, on Saipan, taken before World War II. Many residents were interviewed by Goerner's investigative team to learn if anyone could recall seeing a white woman with short hair captive on the island during the war.

While she was watched all the time and could not go anywhere, Nicholas was able to give the white woman pieces of fruit several times.

One day, according to Nicholas, the woman came out in the yard, looking very sick and sad. When Nicholas gave her a piece of fruit, the white woman gave her a ring from her finger. It was a single pearl set in white gold. The next day one of the police came and got some black cloth from Nicholas' father, a tailor, and had him make some paper flowers. The police said the woman had died of dysentery. Nicholas claims she kept the ring until some time after the war, but it was eventually lost. No one seems to know whether Earhart owned a pearl ring. Photographs of her do not show it. However, Goerner thought it possible that Earhart may have bought such a ring at one of the stops during the around-the-world attempt.

In addition to interviewing eyewitnesses on Saipan, Goerner had located the supposed "Earhart-Noonan" gravesite. He had received maps and photographs from Thomas Devine, a technical sergeant with the 244th Army Postal Unit on Saipan in 1945. Devine claimed to have been walking through a Saipanese cemetery one day when a native woman began to tell him something.

According to Devine, the woman was trying to show him where a white man and woman who had come from the sky had been buried a long time ago. When Devine asked what had happened to the fliers, the woman said that they had been killed by the Japanese. Armed with Devine's photos and instructions, Goerner and several Saipanese located the cemetery and found Devine's landmarks—a variety of gravestones, including a plaster angel with arms raised and a crooked tree. However, Goerner began to question Devine's orientation because he had mislocated the tree on the map. In addition, several of the Saipanese claimed that one of the buildings indicated by Devine on the map was actually south of the cemetery, not north as Devine had shown. Goerner was persuaded to look south and eventually ordered the diggers to work. After two attempts, they had found nothing. Goerner then moved the excavation a few yards closer to the graveyard and ordered the natives to dig once again. About two-and-a-half feet down, they found pieces of skull, shoulder, and leg bones. The total recovery amounted to seven pounds of bones and thirty-seven teeth. Had they found the remains of Earhart and Noonan?

Burial Remains

Before having the remains identified, it was necessary to get permission from Fred Noonan's wife (who had remarried) and Earhart's sister Muriel. It

The cemetery of Garapan, where many grave markers were obscured or buried until the Goerner team excavated in 1963 while attempting to locate the gravesite of Earhart.

was also necessary to get clearance from the U.S. Navy because Saipan had been supervised by the Secretary of the Navy since 1947. While permission was granted quickly by Noonan's wife and Muriel Earhart, the navy took its time. Apparently, in the process of searching Saipan, Goerner had discovered information about secret government activities unrelated to Earhart. The navy wanted to be sure that Goerner could be trusted. After much wrangling, the navy gave clearance in late 1961 to have the remains examined by Dr. Theodore McCown at the University of California at Berkeley. McCown's first guess was that the remains, based on the size of the teeth, represented one man and one woman. As the days passed, the tension grew, waiting for McCown's evaluation. It was another setback. The remains, according to McCown, were not those of the two fliers, but of at least four Asians.

At this point, Goerner was ready to quit. He had no reason to believe that he and his team would ever be able to solve the Earhart mystery. No matter how hard he tried, however, Goerner could not throw in the towel.

The possibility that Earhart was on a spy mission for the U.S. government took root with a letter from John F. Day, a former vice-president of CBS News. Day claimed in his letter to have met a man who had worked on Earhart's plane in California when it had been brought back from Honolulu for repairs. According to this former mechanic, the engines installed in the Electra were twice as powerful as those described in publicity releases. The plane's fuel capacity was also increased, and the range and cruising speed were much longer and higher than the figures released to the public.

Goerner called the former mechanic, who was very cautious on the phone.

The Goerner team removes a skull fragment from one of eight unmarked graves that were excavated on Saipan. None of the remains were ever linked to Earhart or Noonan.

"I can't talk about this business," he said. "I gave my word."

"But you've already talked to some people."

"I know, and I shouldn't have."

"Please answer this...After the special work was done on the Electra, was it capable of flying over the Caroline and Marshall Islands en route to Howland?"

"Yes."

Strange Leads

The idea of a possible spy mission widened further when Vivian Maatta of Oakland, California, came forward. Maatta told Goerner that she had been hired in early 1937 to be Earhart's personal secretary. A man named William Miller, an executive with the Civil Aeronautics Authority in Washington, D.C., did the hiring. Maatta ended up doing more work for Miller and Putnam, Earhart's husband, than for Earhart. According to Maatta, Earhart and Miller had long meetings, pouring over maps. "I'm sure," Maatta told Goerner, "it didn't have anything to do with what they were telling the public." On one occasion, Maatta listened in on a phone conversation Miller was having. "He was ordered to go to Port Darwin, Australia, on some sort of special mission which had to do with Miss Earhart," Maatta said. When Maatta asked Miller if she should type up notes on the phone call (a practice she followed regularly), Miller became very excited and wanted to know how much Maatta had heard. Then Miller told Maatta to forget the whole thing, and not to mention it to anyone. He stressed that his trip was top-secret government business.

Vivian Maatta was Earhart's replacement secretary while Earhart was in Oakland, California. Goerner found the woman who was her regular secretary from 1935 until Earhart's disappearance. She worked then in North Hollywood, California. While the woman was sworn to secrecy, she did tell

This rusted radio direction finder, like the one on Earhart's Electra, was recovered from Saipan in 1961. This led to speculation that Earhart may have flown to Saipan, but the equipment was later verified as Japanese.

Goerner that President Roosevelt knew everything about Earhart's flight. That is why, she said, Roosevelt ordered the U.S. Navy to spend four million dollars in its efforts to find Earhart. Earhart's former secretary also indicated that it was the U.S. government, not Purdue University, that bought Earhart's Electra. Her comments bolstered the idea that Earhart was, indeed, on a spy mission.

On July 18, 1962, the U.S. Coast Guard released what had been until then the classified report of Commander Warner Thompson, the *Itasca* captain in 1937. The report revealed a story of confusion from the moment of the Coast Guard's involvement until the disappearance of Earhart. It criticized everyone from the navy to the Interior Department. If the report had been released in 1937, reporters would have questioned why so many departments of the

Fred Goerner with a piece of airplane wreckage found in Tanapag Harbor, Saipan. Investigators believed the remains of the Lockheed Electra were at the bottom. More of the wreckage is displayed on the opposite page.

government had been involved in what was supposed to be a civilian flight. They might also have questioned why Earhart was so secretive about her radio plans, why her messages to the *Itasca* were so infrequent and incomplete, and why she didn't broadcast on 500 kilocycles so the *Itasca* could use its homing gear. All of these unanswered questions fueled the spy theory.

The Investigation Continues

In 1962 Goerner returned to Saipan, where he interviewed many of the same people he had talked to two years before. One of the men, Vicente Galvan, denied knowing anything about Earhart in 1960. Two years later, he changed his story. According to Galvan, the woman flier and possibly her male navigator were brought to Saipan from the Marshall Islands. They did not, however, fly their own plane to Saipan, but were brought by a Japanese ship. Other Saipanese confirmed Vicente's story. Manuel Sablan heard the Japanese brag about capturing "the woman flier who spies." Sablan claimed to have seen the woman, and his description fit Earhart. Antonio Diaz offered more. "The woman flier," he said, "was brought to Saipan. It is also possible her plane was brought here. The Japanese one day unload it from ship at Tanapag, and they take it on big truck to Aslito Field." When Goerner questioned Diaz about a man with the woman, Diaz said he heard there was a man, but that he did not see him. And when asked what happened to the fliers, Diaz said he did not think they ever left the island.

Joaquina Cabrera did laundry for the Japanese and the prisoners who were held on Saipan in 1937

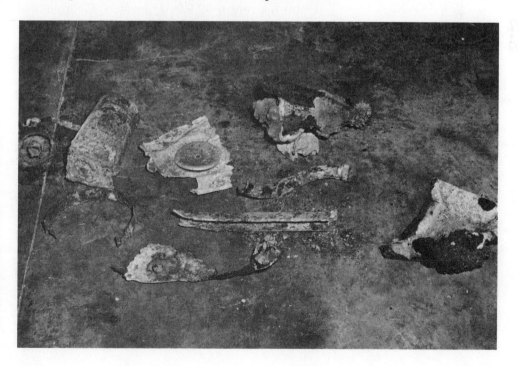

or 1938. She told Goerner that a white lady and man were held at the prison. The woman, Cabrera said, wore a man's clothes when she first came, including pants and a leather jacket. The man's head, said Cabrera, was hurt and covered with a bandage. The police took the man to "another place," and he never came back. According to Cabrera, the woman was thin and very tired. One day, the police told Cabrera that the woman was dead from a disease.

Before Goerner left Saipan in 1962, he concluded that Earhart and Noonan were captured in the Marshall Islands and then brought to Saipan, possibly by the Japanese ship *Kamoi*, which may also have brought their plane. While there was probably more than one woman among the prisoners on Saipan, the description given of the white woman fit Earhart. Goerner also concluded that both Earhart and Noonan died in Saipan and were buried somewhere in the area.

Upon his return to San Francisco, Goerner met Fleet Admiral Chester Nimitz, the former commander of U.S. Naval Forces in the Pacific. It was the first of many meetings in which Nimitz encouraged Goerner to continue his investigation. Goerner was, according to Nimitz, on to something that would "stagger his imagination." Had there been a government coverup of the Earhart incident? Did President Roosevelt and others know what had happened to Earhart and Noonan? In his attempt to answer these questions, Goerner flew to Washington, D.C., where he hoped to get the classified reports on Earhart from the State Department and the Navy Department.

At the State Department, Goerner was told that the records relating to Earhart contained little classified information. However "little" the information, Goerner wanted to see it. What he discovered helped him formulate his final theory. There was, for example, a notation in the file that said the Electra's radio equipment had been carefully repaired and tested during the stop at Port Darwin, Australia. Two other letters indicated that the plane's engines were not those listed in publicity releases to the public, but engines more powerful, capable of a cruising speed of 200 or more miles per hour. In addition, an extra telegraph system had also been installed in the plane to be used in case of an emergency. Did these changes mean that Earhart's plane had been fitted for a mission other than the one announced to the public? Goerner also found a letter in the file, dated March 1944, indicating that a U.S. Navy lieutenant commander had reported learning that an American woman with a male companion had come down near Jaluit in the Marshall Islands several years before the war.

After six years of investigation, Goerner pieced together the thousands of interviews, the four trips to the islands of the Pacific, and the information contained in the Earhart classified files. His account is a reconstruction of what may have happened on that

The graveyard on Saipan where the 1961-63 excavations were done.

The ruins of Garapan prison. This cell was said to be the one where Earhart was kept prisoner.

tragic last leg of the around-the-world flight.

The Goerner Theory

Earhart did not fly directly from Lae, New Guinea, to Howland Island as planned. Instead, says Goerner, she made a secret detour north to the major Japanese base of Truk where she observed from the air the number of airfields there. By the time Earhart reached Truk in the late afternoon, the plane was light enough (having used enough fuel) to climb to its best altitude for speed. The Japanese had never seen a foreign aircraft over Truk and were caught completely by surprise. There were no Japanese planes in the air, so Earhart was able to get all the information she needed.

With the first part of the mission over, Earhart headed for Howland. But the plane ran into clouds, thunderstorms, and heavy winds. Noonan tried to navigate by the stars, but the clouds made seeing them impossible. The plane was too far away to receive signals from the *Itasca* or from the DF antenna on Howland to get a fix on its signals. Besides, if Earhart asked for a bearing too soon, the secret mission might have been discovered. How could she explain why she was flying toward Howland from the northwest instead of the southwest? So, Earhart kept her radio transmissions brief. At 5:15 a.m., Noonan thought they were 200 miles from Howland. Earhart radioed that information to the Itasca and asked for a position. She repeated the request thirty minutes later and said that they were within a hundred miles of the tiny island.

Out of Fuel

By 7:00 a.m., Earhart was sure she had passed Howland in the dark and began to circle. At 8:00 a.m., she received a brief transmission from the *Itasca* but could not get a bearing. About forty minutes later, Noonan used the position of the sun to estimate the plane's location, and Earhart radioed that to the *Itasca*. She then decided to use an emergency plan that had been worked out ahead of time. With no more than two hours of fuel left, she turned back toward the Gilbert Islands controlled by the British. But because she was off course, she was flying instead toward the Japanese-controlled Marshall Islands. With hope of finding land almost gone, Earhart saw a small island. Since the water between the beach and reef was shallow, they decided to risk landing on the water inside the reef. Earhart and Noonan crash-landed at Mili Atoll in the southeastern Marshalls.

Earhart was not hurt, but Noonan had struck his head and was unconscious. As the theory goes,

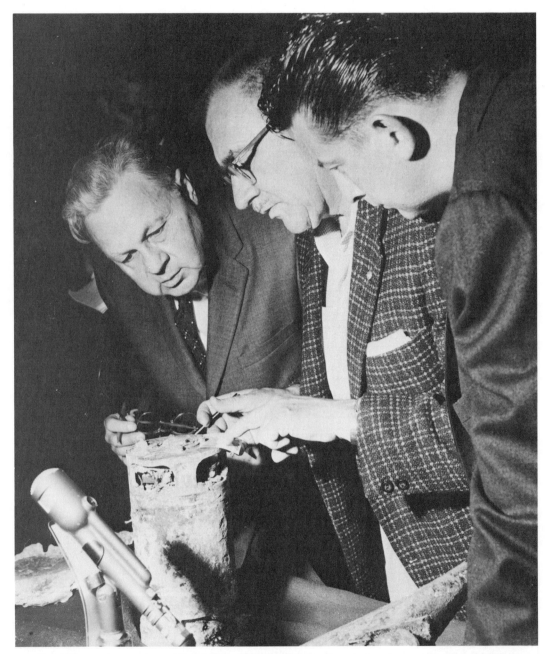

Paul Mantz (center) and Fred Goerner (right) examine the generator recovered from Tanapag Harbor in Saipan.

Earhart bandaged his head and waited for him to regain consciousness. A few minutes later, Noonan awoke but had trouble standing. Earhart began sending SOS messages. And every newspaper in the United States began to carry the story of Earhart's disappearance. Now the race was on to see who would find the missing fliers first—the Americans or the Japanese.

On or about July 13, 1937, a Japanese fishing boat moved into the Marshalls and took Earhart and Noonan prisoners. They were later either transferred to a boat that transported seaplanes or to a survey ship and taken finally to Saipan, Japan's military headquarters in the Pacific. Both Earhart and Noonan later died in Saipan, either from illness or by execution.

Goerner argued that because the fliers knew about Japan's illegal military activities in the Pacific the Japanese could not return them to the United States. And Goerner speculates that the U.S. government suspected what had happened to Earhart and Noonan in 1937 and confirmed it in 1944 when U.S. forces invaded Saipan. After the invasion, President Roosevelt decided not to tell the American public about the fate of Earhart and Noonan because he was running for reelection and did not want to be blamed for not rescuing the two fliers. Following Roosevelt's death, President Harry Truman also decided not to make the details public. Nor were the Japanese interested in disclosing the truth. They would have had to admit their illegal use of the Mandated Islands before World War II. Such a revelation would have meant a violation of international law and further problems for the defeated Japanese.

Did Earhart Escape?

For years after Earhart's disappearance, there were those who thought she might still be alive. A group calling itself "Operation Earhart" investigated and eventually endorsed this theory. Joe Klaas, one of the men who participated in this unofficial investigation, wrote a book in 1970 called *Amelia Earhart Lives*. In it, he claimed Operation Earhart had discovered that a woman living in New Jersey named Irene Bolam was really Amelia Earhart. The author also claimed that Fred Noonan had been located, living under a different name. Though both people looked somewhat like the missing fliers, they strongly denied any connection.

The Operation Earhart Hypothesis

Operation Earhart theorized that Earhart had been on a spy mission similar to the one in the movie *Flight For Freedom*. After the accident in Hawaii that postponed Earhart's around-the-world flight, the theory goes, government officials secretly persuaded Earhart to switch to a new, experimental Electra. The plane looked like the original but was faster and could fly longer distances. Earhart overflew Truk Island and the Marshall Islands, planning to get "lost" on Canton Island, giving the navy an excuse to search the Japanese islands while looking for her. However, something went wrong, and the Japanese forced the Electra down on Hull Island and captured Earhart and Noonan.

According to the theory, they were then taken to Japan where they were held until the end of World War II. Their release supposedly was obtained in exchange for U.S. promises that Emperor Hirohito of Japan would not be tried as a war criminal. Once back in America, Earhart and Noonan were sworn to secrecy. Earhart supposedly assumed the alias Irene Bolam and Noonan assumed the alias William Van Dusen. And what about the airplane? An Electra with the same registration number as the one Earhart flew in 1937 crashed into a California mountain in 1961. Critics concede that much, but contend that the 1961 Electra was a World War II version whose number Paul Mantz had changed in honor of Earhart and her achievements.

To support their claim that Earhart had switched planes, Operation Earhart pointed out differences in the photos taken of the plane at various times during the flight. They noted differences in the hatch, navigation lights, and the plane's registration numbers. Operation Earhart critics contend that these changes were made before the Electra and Earhart attempted the around-the-world flight.

Irene Bolam was so angry about the claims that she was really Earhart that she threatened to sue McGraw-Hill, the publishers of *Amelia Earhart Lives*. McGraw-Hill withdrew the book from circulation, but not before many people were swayed to believe that Amelia Earhart was still alive.

"Japan was preparing itself for war. When would Japan strike against the United States? How advanced were her bases in the Mandates? …those questions had to be answered on a reconnaissance mission, almost parallel to the U-2 flight of the 1960s."

Fred Goerner, *The Search for Amelia Earhart*

"The aircraft would have been over the 'target' in the middle of the night when cameras would be useless; there was no infrared equipment in those days, and use of photoflash would have given Earhart away immediately."

Vincent Loomis, *Amelia Earhart: The Final Story*

Five

Was Earhart an Innocent Victim?

One day in 1967, Air Force pilot Vincent Loomis picked up a copy of *Reader's Digest* and read about Goerner's spy theory. It fascinated Loomis. What if the Electra had not fallen into the ocean near Howland Island? How much fuel would have been left for it to land somewhere else? Could Earhart have flown to another island in the Pacific and crash-landed? Loomis was confused by the conflicting reports he had read. Various theories had placed Earhart and Noonan in Saipan, the Marshalls, Turk, and Hull Island. They could not have been in so many places at the same time.

Loomis began his own investigation into the fate of Amelia Earhart. It lasted almost twenty years. It took him and others to the Marshall Islands many times, as well as to Japan. Using personal interviews, ship logs, computer technology, and U.S. Navy files, Loomis's investigation reached many of the same conclusions as Goerner. There is, however, one major exception: Loomis contends that Earhart was not a spy. Instead, she was headed for Howland Island but got lost. Since she had flown over the Mandated Islands, an area where the Japanese were

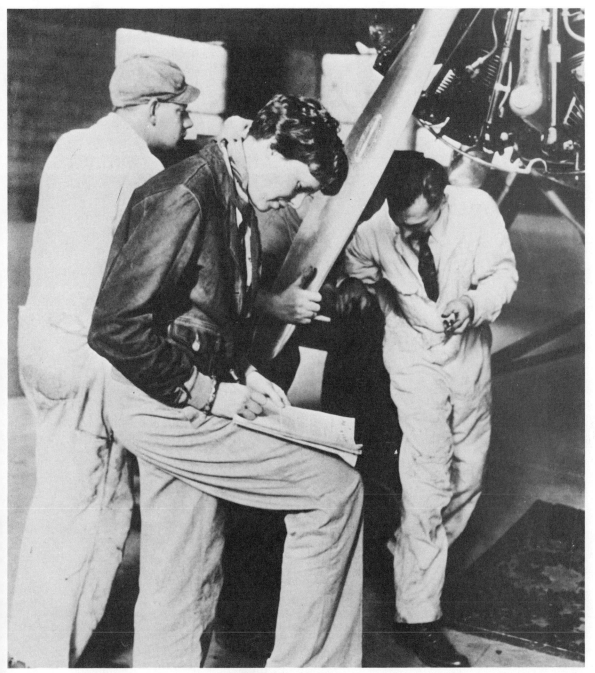

Earhart in Honolulu.

secretly operating militarily, Earhart was taken for a spy and imprisoned. Fourteen months later, a Saipanese woman was asked to provide some burial wreaths. When the woman asked what had happened, she was told that the "American woman" had died of *sekiri*, the Japanese word for dysentery. Noonan had been killed earlier after losing his temper and throwing a bowl of soup at his Japanese captors.

A New Investigation

During his first trip to the Marshall Islands in 1978, Loomis talked to the vice chairman of the Marshall Islands Political Status Committee. Tony DeBrum was very certain about Earhart having landed in the Marshalls. "We all know about this woman who was reported to have come down on Mili southeast of Majuro, was captured by the Japanese, and taken off to Jaluit," he said. DeBrum suggested that Loomis look up a few of the Marshallese who might have seen something firsthand. Unfortunately, none of the people interviewed had actually seen an American plane or crew in the years before World War II, the time in which Earhart attempted her around-the-world flight. Many of them said, however, that Japanese friends had talked about a lady pilot who landed near Mili, a few hundred miles away. To find out if there was any truth to what these people reported, eyewitnesses had to be found.

On his next trip to the Marshalls in July 1979, Loomis interviewed a Marshallese fisherman who, along with another man, had supposedly seen Earhart crash. The fisherman and his now dead friend saw an airplane land on the reef about 200 feet offshore. Frightened, they hid in the jungle and remained there until they saw what they thought were two men get out of the plane into a yellow boat and come ashore. The Japanese soon arrived by boat and started to question the two fliers. During the questioning, the Japanese started to slap the fliers.

One of them screamed. It was then that they realized one of the fliers was a woman.

The old fisherman's friend said that he saw the fliers bury a silver metal box before their captors arrived. They buried it under a kanal tree. Could the "metal box" have been the tin box that Noonan had carried with him aboard the Electra before taking off from Lae—the only piece of personal luggage he had with him? If the box could be recovered and its contents verified, would it serve as proof that Earhart and Noonan had ditched in the Marshall Islands?

Loomis and his search party sailed to the area where the fisherman said the plane had ditched on a reef 200 feet offshore. They tried to locate the kanal tree under which the "metal box" was supposedly buried. The two metal detectors they used turned out to be very ineffective, and there were dozens of

After the crash that ended Earhart's first attempt at a global flight, the Lockheed Electra was repaired and the flight plan changed so that Earhart and Noonan would fly east instead of west. Note the direction finder mounted above the cockpit.

Earhart may have ditched her plane near an atoll such as this one.

kanal trees. If anything was going to be found among the dense overgrowth on the island, more sophisticated gear and a clearer idea of the right tree would be needed.

After this second trip to the Marshalls, another American joined Loomis on his latest Earhart investigation. His name was Paul Rafford, Jr., a communications and astronaut recovery expert with the U.S. space program during the 1960s and 1970s. Rafford was interested in using space-age computer techniques to find out what went wrong on Earhart's flight. He wanted to find out how Earhart's radio navigation failed her. And he wanted to know why a man of Noonan's ability had not been able to use the radios to get the Electra to Howland. To find answers, Rafford built a scale radio, matching the characteristics of Earhart's Electra. Frequencies, power, and antennas were exactly like the Electra's. After operating the model countless times, learning the exact transmission strength characteristics of the Electra's radio, Rafford fed the findings into a computer.

Rafford went to Washington, D.C., to review the files of the navy's archives and the Smithsonian Institution's National Air and Space Museum (NASM). There he discovered many new pieces of the Earhart puzzle. A historian, Dr. Francis Holdbrook, had corresponded with Harry Balfour, the radio operator on Lae, New Guinea who talked with Earhart during the first eight hours of the flight. According to Balfour, Earhart had not followed a direct route from Lae to Howland as planned. Neither had she followed a route that would allow her to spy on the Japanese. Instead, she had decided to fly by way of Nauru Island to reach Howland.

In 1983 Rafford made another visit to the NASM library. He signed out all of the library's microfilm records on Amelia Earhart. Rafford found what he was looking for—the actual message radioed to Earhart from Nauru. In it, the Nauru radio operator confirmed that giant phosphate-mining lights would be kept on all night and could be seen as far as thirty-four miles away. That way, Earhart could not miss Nauru as she approached the island after sunset.

A Different Flight Plan

Why had Earhart decided to change her flight? According to Balfour, Earhart felt she could not trust Noonan to navigate. He had started drinking again. Earhart felt it necessary to take the navigation into her own hands. If she left Lae between 9:00 and 11:00 a.m., Earhart could navigate during the day using island sightings. Then she could turn toward Nauru with a good chance of sighting it in the dark because of its bright lights. After leaving Nauru, she would have no checkpoints to guide her before reaching Howland. But at sunrise she could get a position by having Noonan shoot a sunline, if he was up to it, or by using his *Nautical Almanac*. This would give Earhart an idea of how far she was from

Was Earhart the victim of poor navigation and inadequate radio training?

Howland but not necessarily whether she was on course or not. Earhart had reportedly tried to get Balfour to take Noonan's place on the flight between Lae and Howland. He knew how to use the radios and had lived in the Pacific most of his life. Balfour apparently considered the idea but eventually turned Earhart down. He said he felt the flight was doomed and remained in Lae.

After takeoff from Lae, Earhart radioed hourly reports to Balfour for eight hours. After passing Nukumanu Islands, she headed toward Nauru Island, 600 miles northeast. An hour later, Balfour talked with Earhart for the last time. But the head of police on Nauru heard Earhart on his own home shortwave receiver as she approached and then passed the island. "Lights in sight ahead," he heard her say. Earhart had reached the halfway point between Lae and Howland. There were more than 1,100 miles to go.

Poor Communication

Early in the morning, the radiomen aboard the *Itasca* heard Earhart for the first time. It was the beginning of a very frustrating and confusing series of events. The *Itasca's* radio operators realized they were trying to guide a crew safely toward Howland that had not even a basic knowledge of radio. The confusion, Loomis wrote in his book, was as "simple as a modern-day radio listener trying to tune in an AM radio station by using a number on the FM band." Earhart requested 7,500 kilocycles, while the channel she most likely wanted was 400 kilocycles, or 750 meters, a standard direction-finding frequency. With only a minimal knowledge of radio, it would not have been hard to get the two mixed up. Without accurate radio direction-finding, the only way to find Howland would be a sun line. Noonan shot the line and Earhart reported it: "We are on the line of position one-five-seven dash three-three-seven.... We are running north and south." If Earhart had been anywhere within thirty miles of Howland, she would have seen clouds of black smoke coming from the *Itasca*.

But when Earhart radioed, "We must be on you but cannot see you," she was, according to Rafford, 150 miles north-northwest of Howland, hopelessly off course. Unable to find Howland, Earhart followed her emergency plan. She had told William Miller before the flight, "If we don't pick up Howland, I'll try to fly back into the Gilberts and

"It was told by the crew on that ship that they found them somewhere between Gilbert Islands and Mili Island, and we treat the man, I personally did…At this same time I saw, they told me, their plane. It was on the back side of the ship."

Bilimon Amaran

"I have a hunch they are sitting somewhere on a coral island…Fred's probably out sitting on a rock now catching their dinner with those fishing lines they had aboard."

George Putnam (after the Electra's disappearance)

find a nice stretch of beach." Earhart thought she was near Howland and plotted a course west for the Gilberts. But, as this theory goes, she was far north and went straight for the Marshall Islands instead.

Did Anyone See Earhart?

After tracing the probable path of Earhart's final flight, Loomis needed a firsthand account of her fate from the Japanese. If they could confirm what Rafford suspected, the Earhart mystery could be solved.

Bilimon Amaran had been a medical corpsman with the Japanese Navy before and during World War II. After the war, he settled in the Marshalls where he made his living as a store owner. Amaran was known for his kindness, and it was rumored that he had had some actual contact with the lady pilot.

What Amaran reported to Loomis turned out to be a most important puzzle piece. Sometime during 1937, Amaran said, he was working at the Japanese military hospital on Jaluit in the Marshall Islands when he was asked to go with the director of health services to a Japanese military ship. When he got to the ship, Amaran saw a white man and woman. The man was wounded in the front of his head and also in his leg. Amaran said that he personally treated the man and that, while the head wound was not very serious, the one around the knee was deep, inflamed, and bleeding slightly. Amaran was told that the crew had found the two fliers somewhere near Mili Island. He also saw their plane on the back of the ship, still in the canvas slings that pulled it from the water. One of the wings was broken. When asked if he knew where the two fliers were taken, Amaran said he was told that the ship was going to leave Jaluit and head to Truk, then Saipan and maybe Japan.

Back in Saipan, Loomis talked to a man who remembered seeing "a white woman in the back of a truck with Japanese men with her." He later heard from friends that the woman had been taken from

the water after a plane had crashed. Did this mean that Earhart had not made it all the way to Saipan in the Electra? Could she have landed somewhere else, been put aboard a Japanese ship, and then transferred to a Japanese plane for the journey to Saipan?

If the Japanese ships in the Marshalls in the summer of 1937 could be traced, maybe there would be some definite information about how Earhart ended up in Saipan. In the fall of 1981, Loomis uncovered a central intelligence document on Amelia Earhart in the National Air and Space Museum files. Dated August 1949, the document detailed the U.S. government's attempts to get as much information as it could from the Japanese about Earhart's disappearance. American intelligence agents were reportedly

Even if Earhart survived the plane crash and made it to an island, finding her would have been extremely difficult for both the American and the Japanese forces.

The last known photograph of Earhart and Noonan, taken just before their takeoff from Lae, New Guinea.

unable to find any Japanese Navy records about Earhart, but interviews were carried out with Japanese personnel who had supposedly searched for the Electra after it was lost on the way to Howland. According to the document, the Japanese Navy's 12th Squadron was instructed to send the *Kamoi*, a seaplane tender, and several large boats to the south of Jaluit to search for Earhart. Later the survey ship *Koshu* was ordered into the area. The Japanese testified that the *Kamoi* led the rescue effort, but no traces of Earhart were found. The investigation was closed.

In December 1981, Loomis went to Japan to interview Jyuichi Hirabayashi, who had served aboard the *Kamoi*, and to locate what records could be found. Loomis and his interpreter found a book on Japanese naval ships. The book listed the *Kamoi* docked in Japan by July 10, 1937, only eight days after Earhart's plane went down. Loomis suspected that the *Kamoi* could not have taken part in the search as reported to American intelligence in 1949. The *Koshu* was listed as a coal-burning survey ship, assigned to the Marshall Islands in July 1937. Could the *Koshu* have been the ship that Bilimon Amaran boarded?

Jyuichi Hirabayashi had served aboard the *Kamoi* from early 1936 through July 10, 1937. He had responded to an ad that Loomis had placed in several Japanese newspapers, seeking *Kamoi* personnel. Hirabayashi came to meet Loomis soon after he arrived in Japan, bringing the ship's log entries, numerous papers, and a collection of photos from his tour. Hirabayashi confirmed that the *Kamoi* was nowhere near the Marshall Islands when the Electra went down. The ship was docked in Saipan, leaving on July 4 for Ise Bay, Japan, where it docked on July 10. The Japanese had apparently lied to the United States.

Hirabayashi then provided the names of the four

ships in the Japanese Navy's 12th Squadron that supposedly combed the water south of Jaluit for the missing Electra. All four ships, including the *Kamoi*, were docked in the home islands. None had participated in the search. The *Koshu*, however, had not been a part of the 12th Squadron. It was reportedly anchored at Ponape in the Caroline Islands, where it was ordered to proceed to the Marshall Islands and "search" for Earhart and the missing Electra. But the ship's log entries revealed no search efforts. Again, Loomis concluded, the Japanese had lied.

Where did the *Koshu* go, if it did not "search" the waters south of Jaluit for Earhart? According to Loomis, who pieced together interviews and message traffic reports between Japan and its diplomatic offices, the *Koshu* went straight to Jaluit and anchored there on July 13. The ship left Jaluit for several days, picked up Earhart and Noonan where they had ditched the Electra near the island of Mili Mili, and then returned to Jaluit. It was then that Bilimon Amaran boarded the vessel and treated Noonan. After Amaran and his companions left the ship, it reportedly sailed for Truk and Saipan on July 19, the date the Japanese government said it gave up its search for Earhart. Hirabayashi remembered that the *Koshu* did not have any ship doctors. It made sense that Amaran and his superior had been called aboard to treat Noonan.

The Loomis Theory

What would the Japanese have wanted with Earhart? And why would they have kept her rescue a secret, if, indeed, they had found her? Records from Japanese government sources indicated that the Japanese were watching Earhart's flight very closely. The government was particularly interested in the flight as it got closer to the Marshall Islands, where the Japanese had begun to illegally build their military strength. When the world press reported that the

Electra was missing, the Japanese were concerned. They did not want the United States searching for the plane in the Marshalls. Japan refused to let Americans search the area, saying that they would conduct their own search.

According to Loomis, Earhart thought she was south of Howland when she was really northwest. Unable to see the island or the *Itasca* after circling and trying to make contact by radio, she decided to turn around and fly the 400 miles back to the Gilbert Islands. Without knowing it, Earhart and Noonan were heading straight into the Japanese-controlled Marshall Islands. After flying for more than four-and-a-half hours with nothing in sight, Earhart knew she would have to land wherever she could. Fuel was low, and she was hopelessly lost. Descending, Earhart tried to pick out a stretch of land. All she saw were small islands that looked to be covered by trees. Her only alternative was to land on top of one of the reefs in the water surrounding the islands. Earhart had been through crash landings before, but she had never had to ditch a plane in the water.

The Japanese, Loomis suggests, heard the Electra as it approached the reef surrounding the island of Mili Mili and manned a small fishing boat toward the spot where they had last seen the plane. Soon after, the Japanese fishing boat arrived, and the Japanese military personnel on board ran toward the fliers. They started to question Earhart and Noonan, but the language barrier prevented any communication. Frustrated, one of the Japanese began to slap the shorter of the two fliers, who let out a high-pitched scream. The "man" was a woman.

On July 14 the *Koshu* headed for Mili Mili to pick up the Electra and the captured fliers. Because Noonan needed medical attention, the ship returned to Jaluit where there was a military hospital. The director of health services and Amaran were allowed on the ship to treat Noonan. On July 19 the *Koshu*

"The thing that was uppermost in her memory was the fact that two people were white and she had never seen white people before, coupled with the fact that the woman was wearing pants and had cut her hair short."

Clyde E. Holley, an attorney who handled Amelia Earhart's legal affairs, talking about Josephine Blanco Akiyama

"On numerous occasions, the Navy has conducted thorough investigations in order to verify the many rumors over the years that Miss Earhart and Mr. Noonan were on Saipan or its vicinity. None of these investigations have uncovered any information which could conceivably substantiate either of them having been on this island."

Rear Admiral G.R. Donaho, Director of Naval Administration

Noonan and Earhart may have flown off course toward the Marshall Islands. If so, they may have ended up in this Saipan cell block, mistaken for spies by the Japanese.

sailed for Truk, where Earhart and Noonan were transferred to a Japanese Navy seaplane and flown to Saipan. Eleven-year-old Josephine Akiyama saw a large, two-motored plane fly overhead and then disappear near the harbor. It was then that she ran to the beach, where she found a large group gathered around the two. Though Josephine thought she had seen the seaplane ditch, Loomis contends that the plane had simply landed and that Earhart and Noonan were taken for questioning and locked up in Garapan Prison. The Japanese feared that the

Americans had seen enough Japanese military activity to expose their violation of international law.

According to Akiyama's brother-in-law, Grigorio Camarcho, Noonan began to resist his Japanese captors as the weeks passed into months. He and Earhart were given little to eat and both became ill with dysentery. As the theory goes, Noonan finally lost his temper and threw a bowl of soup at his captors. He was taken out of his prison cell and executed.

Earhart's health worsened. According to many eyewitnesses, including Matilde Nicholas (interviewed first by Fred Goerner), Earhart died of dysentery fourteen months after she was captured by the Japanese.

Six

Has a Gravesite Ever Been Found?

Just when the American public might have thought that everything that could be known about the disappearance of Amelia Earhart had been discovered, former Army sergeant Thomas Devine (who had served on Saipan between 1944 and 1945) published his own account of the Earhart mystery. In *Eyewitness: The Amelia Earhart Incident*, Devine claims that the CBS investigation led by Fred Goerner was incomplete. Devine said he saw Earhart's plane three times in 1944 at Aslito Field in Saipan. The last time he saw the Electra, the plane was burning. A year later, Devine met an Okinawan woman who showed him an unmarked grave. She insisted that a white man and woman were buried there, saying that they had "come from the sky." Over forty years of research have convinced Devine that this was the grave of Amelia Earhart and Fred Noonan.

Devine's information, if valid, would support those who believe that Earhart was off course and was taken to Saipan by the Japanese where she and her navigator died. His account would also support those who claim that the U.S. government knew

The brave aviator believed her around-the-world attempt would be
the most important of her career.

A bombed-out building in Garapan, following the invasion of U.S. forces in 1944. Thomas Devine (below) was stationed on Saipan at this time and claims he saw Earhart's missing Electra.

more about Earhart's fate than it ever admitted to the American people.

Saipan was the headquarters for the Japanese Central Pacific Area Fleet. On June 11, 1944, a United States Navy carrier force began a 96 hour naval and air bombardment of Saipan. Three days later, battleships under the command of Vice Admiral Richmond Kelley Turner attacked Saipan from the sea. Known as "The Great Marianas Turkey Shoot," the carrier battle at sea and an air battle over Saipan downed 500 Japanese planes. The Japanese Fleet was broken and retreated. After more land battles, the entire southern portion of Saipan fell under American control on June 26. It was not long before the Americans captured the entire island.

One of the Japanese prisoners was reportedly questioned by a Sgt. Ralph R. Kanna. The prisoner supposedly had on him a photograph of Amelia Earhart standing near Japanese aircraft on an airfield. Through an interpreter, the captured soldier told Kanna that the woman in the photograph and a male companion had been taken prisoner by the Japanese. He thought both had later been executed. Kanna did not keep the photograph. He did, however, report the photograph to the Regimental Intelligence Officer.

A Mysterious Encounter

When Devine's 244th army unit came ashore, the fighting on Saipan had ended. One day, Devine was told to drive a commanding officer to Aslito Field. As they approached the airfield, they could see that security was very tight. A military policeman (MP) refused to let them proceed, instructing the men to take another route to the airfield. Devine's commanding officer reported to the administration building, while Devine waited outside. During the wait, he saw a marine officer yelling at a man in a white shirt. The marine was angry about the tight security. "We know Earhart's plane is in there," the marine yelled. "What are you trying to pull? Our men laid their lives on the line, and now they won't even get credit for finding the plane!"

After the marine and the man in the white shirt went into the administration building, Devine talked to one of the guards, asking if Earhart's plane was really inside. "Yes," the guard said. "But for the love of God don't say I said so! I don't know why the hell they want to keep it a secret."

Some hours later, Devine heard a big roar of airplane motors from Aslito Field. "Suddenly," he wrote, "there was a deafening roar overhead. There, flying right above us, was a large, twin-engine, double-fin civilian plane. It maneuvered a bit awkwardly as it went in for a landing at Aslito Field. From the ground, I could easily read the identification number—NR 16020."

That night, Devine and another soldier decided to chance an unauthorized visit to Aslito Field to see what they could find. They found the twin-engine

The Okinawan woman who supposedly showed Devine the Earhart-Noonan gravesite.

plane. As the two approached the plane, a photographer who was apparently taking pictures ran away. He was too far away for Devine to determine whether he was military or civilian. Devine got closer to the plane and noticed that the left tire was flat. At the tail was the identification number he had memorized earlier—NR 16020. Devine and his friend decided to get into the plane. As the two looked for an entry on the right side of the plane, Devine turned and saw the photographer behind him, looking as if he had just snapped a picture. He ran away once again. Two men came out from another hangar. One of the men was the man in the white shirt Devine had seen earlier in the day. Nervous, Devine and his friend fled.

Not long after, Devine heard a muffled explosion at Aslito Field and saw a fire. He went to investigate. When he could see what was burning, he was amazed. The twin-engine plane was engulfed in flames. After the flames died down, Devine returned to his base and wrote down the serial number of the plane—NR 16020.

Devine decided not to say anything about what he had seen. He was aware of the secrecy surrounding the airfield and did not want to press his luck. Devine is convinced that he arrived at the airfield during the final preparations to destroy Earhart's plane. He speculates that the original plans called for ditching the plane at sea after dark, but that either the plane's flat tire or his having seen the plane may have caused a change. Two or three weeks after the burning, Devine was mulling over the events of his first day on Saipan, and realized that he recognized the man in the white shirt. He claims it was Secretary of the Navy James Forrestal!

Who Would Destroy the Plane?

Why would Earhart's plane be destroyed in secret? Why would Forrestal not have reported the

discovery of the plane to the world? As Devine sees it, news of Earhart's plane on an island controlled by the Japanese before World War II could have created even more anger toward the defeated Japanese, something the U.S. wanted to control to minimize postwar problems. If the American people then heard stories about the poor treatment of Earhart and Noonan as political prisoners, they would have insisted on the truth. And what would all of this say about the U.S. Navy and the Coast Guard? Why had they failed to find the fliers in 1937? Why had the search been conducted so far from Saipan? How could the American military have allowed Earhart and Noonan to be captured by the Japanese? If Secretary of the Navy Forrestal had any hopes of winning support for those postwar policies, surmises Devine, he could never say anything about what had

This photograph shows the temporary cemetery on Saipan where Devine claims Earhart and Noonan were buried.

Secretary of the Navy, James V. Forrestal. Was he on Saipan when Earhart's plane was reportedly found?

happened on Saipan. Unfortunately, Forrestal could not be questioned about his possible involvement in the burning of Earhart's plane. He died on May 22, 1949, apparently by suicide.

After Thomas Devine witnessed the burning plane at Aslito Field and identified the man in the white shirt, he spent a year on Saipan with the 244th Postal Unit. His many responsibilities, Devine says, kept him busy and his mind off the Earhart mystery. That all changed one day in 1945 when he and Pfc. John Boggs explored the Chamorro, a native cemetery on Saipan. Boggs photographed many of the sights. While standing in the cemetery, Devine saw an Okinawan woman hanging out laundry. This was the woman who would show Devine the alleged grave. The woman kept lifting her long, black hair to chop at her neck with the side of her hand. What was

she trying to say? Was she acting out a beheading?
Was she trying to show a woman with short hair?
When Devine asked the woman how the white man
and woman came to Saipan, she pointed up and said
they had "come from the sky."

The woman grabbed Devine's arms and pulled
him over to a site and pointed to the ground. The site
was approximately 100 yards north and slightly west
of the Chamorro cemetery. Facing east, Devine
could see some of Saipan's hills in the background.
The site was near a spot along the old main road that
Devine had photographed earlier with Boggs's cam-
era—between the old road and the beach. Devine
decided to ask the woman exactly where the white
man and woman were buried. The woman, reports
Devine, fell on her knees and said, "They are buried

Devine (right) and
investigators trying to find
the exact location of the
alleged gravesite.

here, beneath us!"

"Who buried them?" Devine asked.

"The Japanese killed them," she answered.

A few days after meeting the woman, Devine learned that the Chamorro cemetery was being excavated. He assumed that the interpreter had informed his superiors about the unmarked gravesite the Okinawan woman had identified, and that the American military police were digging in the hopes of finding Earhart and Noonan. Devine later learned that the military police uncovered a military aviator's grave about 1,000 yards north of the gravesite he had been shown. The corpse of a red-headed man was found decapitated. Fred Noonan did not have red hair; the remains of a white woman were not found. On August 12, 1945, Japan surrendered. Devine received orders to report to the replacement depot for his return to the United States. At the depot, Devine claims a naval intelligence officer came up to him and said, "You know about Amelia Earhart!" The man attempted to put Devine on a plane for Hawaii where he would be questioned. Nervous and unwilling to share what he knew, Devine denied that he knew anything about Earhart and was eventually allowed to return to the United States by boat.

Devine tried to get permission to return to Saipan on several occasions, but the navy, then in charge of Saipan, denied his requests. Then in 1961, Fred Goerner, the head of the CBS investigation into Earhart's disappearance, was contacted by Devine. Devine wanted to go with Goerner and his team but the navy told him he could not. While still trying to get permission to return to Saipan on his own, Devine decided to tell Goerner what he knew, in case his request was refused again. Not until 1966 did Devine find out that Goerner and his team had not excavated the right site and, of course, had not found the remains of Earhart and Noonan. Contrary

Another view of the Saipanese cemetery.

to Devine's map and directions, they had excavated an area on the south side of the Chamorro cemetery instead of the north side.

The Devine Theory

In 1963 Devine finally got permission to visit Saipan. He accompanied Fred Goerner and planned to help him locate the correct "Earhart-Noonan" gravesite. From the start, things did not go well. Goerner, he says, was unwilling to talk much or to answer most of his questions. He and Devine spent little time together once they got to Saipan. While searching for the gravesite on his own, Devine located what he was convinced was a temporary graveyard just south of the actual gravesite. There were many changes since Devine had served on Saipan in

This photograph of Earhart was erroneously cited as evidence that she had been taken prisoner by the Japanese. The bracelet on her wrist was mistaken for handcuffs. The picture had been taken years before her disappearance.

1945. The overgrown jungle and a beach road built after the war altered the way everything looked. But Devine searched until he found the crooked tree, the one with the stone wrapped around the trunk, that he had located on the map he had sent to Goerner. Devine was sure he had, at last, found the gravesite he had been looking for! But Devine was reluctant to tell Goerner. He did not feel he could trust Goerner after the way he acted. Devine photographed the tree with the stone trunk, the gravesite along the beach road, and the ruins of a former Japanese jail. He then decided not to tell Goerner what he had found. The day Devine and Goerner were to leave Saipan, Goerner told Devine to go home without him but would not explain why he was staying. As they parted, Devine told Goerner that he would return one day with his own expedition. Very disappointed, Devine left Saipan alone.

After he had returned to the United States, Devine learned in San Francisco that Goerner had dug up the graves of eight people. Devine says that he wrote Goerner for details but that he never heard from him again. Only after reading Goerner's book, *The Search For Amelia Earhart*, did Devine find out that none of the remains Goerner had dug up were that of Earhart or Noonan.

After more than forty years, Devine is still convinced he can find the unmarked grave. "I am determined to return to Saipan…and appeal to readers to join me…by supplying any documents, foreign or domestic, which have bearing on the disappearance of Amelia Earhart, her navigator Fred Noonan, or their Lockheed Electra. The challenge is there and the burden of proof is ours to share."

"Father Sylvan and I quickly noticed that Devine appeared to be wrong about the directions of the cemetery. His diagram showed the entrance facing west…The entrance to the graveyard actually faced north."

Fred Goerner, *The Search for Amelia Earhart*

"Goerner's suspicion arose because I had mislocated the odd-crotched tree on my map-diagram, although the tree was not critical to locating the Earhart-Noonan gravesite."

Thomas Devine, *Eyewitness: The Amelia Earhart Incident*

Conclusion

Will We Ever Know?

There have been books, films, television shows, and countless articles about the disappearance of Amelia Earhart. Theories make her into everything from an American spy captured by the Japanese to an unlucky pilot who crash-landed into the Pacific Ocean. If Earhart was indeed taken prisoner instead of being lost at sea, there is still a faint possibility that human remains, government records, or even journals written by America's best-known female pilot may yet be found. If Earhart and Noonan died in Saipan as many witnesses contend, the chance of uncovering their grave still exists. Such documentable evidence could finally solve the mystery that has captured the imaginations of so many for more than fifty years.

In the meantime, without verifiable evidence, there is no doubt that the debate over what really happened to Amelia Earhart on her flight from Lae to Howland will continue. Did she change her flight plan without letting those monitoring the flight know? Was she forced to ditch the Electra in the Marshalls? Could her "flying laboratory" have been found by United States troops on Saipan during

Earhart never seemed to mind the countless times she was asked
to pose in front of her airplanes.

The cornerstone above was laid in 1937 on Howland, the beginning of construction on the Earhart Lighthouse. The memorial would help ships locate the tiny island.

World War II? Did the United States government cover up the details of the Earhart disappearance by destroying her plane and not disclosing the truth to the American public?

It has been more than half a century since Amelia Earhart, Fred Noonan, and the Electra vanished without a trace. Despite the passage of time, the events on July 2, 1937, continue to fascinate because the disappearance of this brave and sensitive pilot stunned people all over the world. The disappearance of Amelia Earhart remains aviation's most perplexing and intriguing mystery.

For Further Exploration

Melinda Blau, *Whatever Happened to Amelia Earhart?* Milwaukee: Raintree, 1977.

Paul Briand, *Daughter of the Sky.* New York: Duell, Sloan and Pearce, 1960.

Fern G. Brown, *Amelia Earhart Takes Off.* Niles, IL: A. Whitman, 1985.

Roxane Chadwick, *Amelia Earhart: Aviation Pioneer.* Minneapolis: Lerner Publications Company, 1987.

Adele Louise De Leeuw, *Story of Amelia Earhart.* New York: Grosset, 1955.

Amelia Earhart, *The Fun Of It.* New York: Harcourt Brace and Company, 1932.

Doris Shannon Garst, *Amelia Earhart: Heroine of the Skies.* New York: Julian Messner, 1947.

James Moore Howe, *Amelia Earhart: Kansas Girl.* New York: Bobbs, Merrill, 1950.

Valerie Moolman and editors, *Women Aloft.* Alexandria, VA: Time-Life Books, 1981.

John Parlin, *Amelia Earhart: Pioneer In The Sky.* West Haven, CT: Pendulum, 1979.

Blythe Randolph, *Amelia Earhart.* New York: Watts, 1987.

Francene Sabin, Amelia Earhart: *Adventures In The Sky.* Mahwah, NJ: Troll, 1983.

Lillee D. Zierau, *Amelia Earhart: Leading Lady Of The Air Age.* Charlotteville, NY: SamHar Press, 1972.

Additional Bibliography

Jean L. Backus, *Letters From Amelia*. Boston: Beacon Press, 1982.

Thomas E. Devine, *Eyewitness: The Amelia Earhart Incident*. Frederick, CO: Renaissance House, 1987.

Fred Goerner, *The Search For Amelia Earhart*. Garden City, NY: Doubleday & Company, 1966.

Joe Klaas, *Amelia Earhart Lives*. New York: McGraw-Hill, 1970.

Vincent Loomis, *Amelia Earhart: The Final Story*. New York: Random House, 1985.

Index

About the Author

Jane Leder, a freelance writer and author, majored in English at the University of Michigan. She earned her M.A. in American Literature from Roosevelt University in Chicago.

Jane has written books, magazine and newspaper articles, films and videos on a variety of subjects, including AIDS, psychics, pregnancy, and siblings. Her book on teenage suicide, *Dead Serious*, was published in hardcover by Atheneum and in paperback by Avon.

Jane is currently working on a book about brothers and sisters. She lives in Chicago, Illinois, with her husband and teenage son. She enjoys travel, dance, film, and walking.

Picture Credits

UPI/Bettmann Newsphotos, 9, 16, 91, 103
FPG International, 13, 15 (top), 17, 34
The Schlesinger Library, Radcliffe College, 14, 15 (bottom), 21, 24, 43
The Bettmann Archive, 18, 22 (top), 29, 46, 104
Mary Evans Picture Library/Photo Researchers, Inc., 19, 20 (bottom)
Culver Pictures, Inc., 20 (top), 22 (bottom), 80
National Air and Space Museum, 23, 32, 33, 35, 38, 39, 47, 104
National Archives, 25, 40, 57
AP/Wide World Photos, 26, 45, 53, 55, 70, 77, 78, 83, 84
Flying Fish Studio, 30-31
Claude E. Hartford/National Air and Space Museum, 36
Photo Research International, 48
U.S. Naval Historical Center, 50, 96
Frederick Goerner, 54, 58, 60, 61, 63, 64, 67, 68, 75, 88, 92 (bottom), 97, 100
U.S. Navy/Frederick Goerner, 65
Thomas E. Devine, 92 (top), 94, 95, 99